# Think About it!

written by Jenny Alexander

illustrated by Sarah Warburton

# Contents

# Introduction

Sometimes, your mum or dad is not around to tell you what to do, for example when you're playing in the garden or at the park. Then you have to make your own decisions. Don't always do the first thing that comes into your head.

# Going to the park

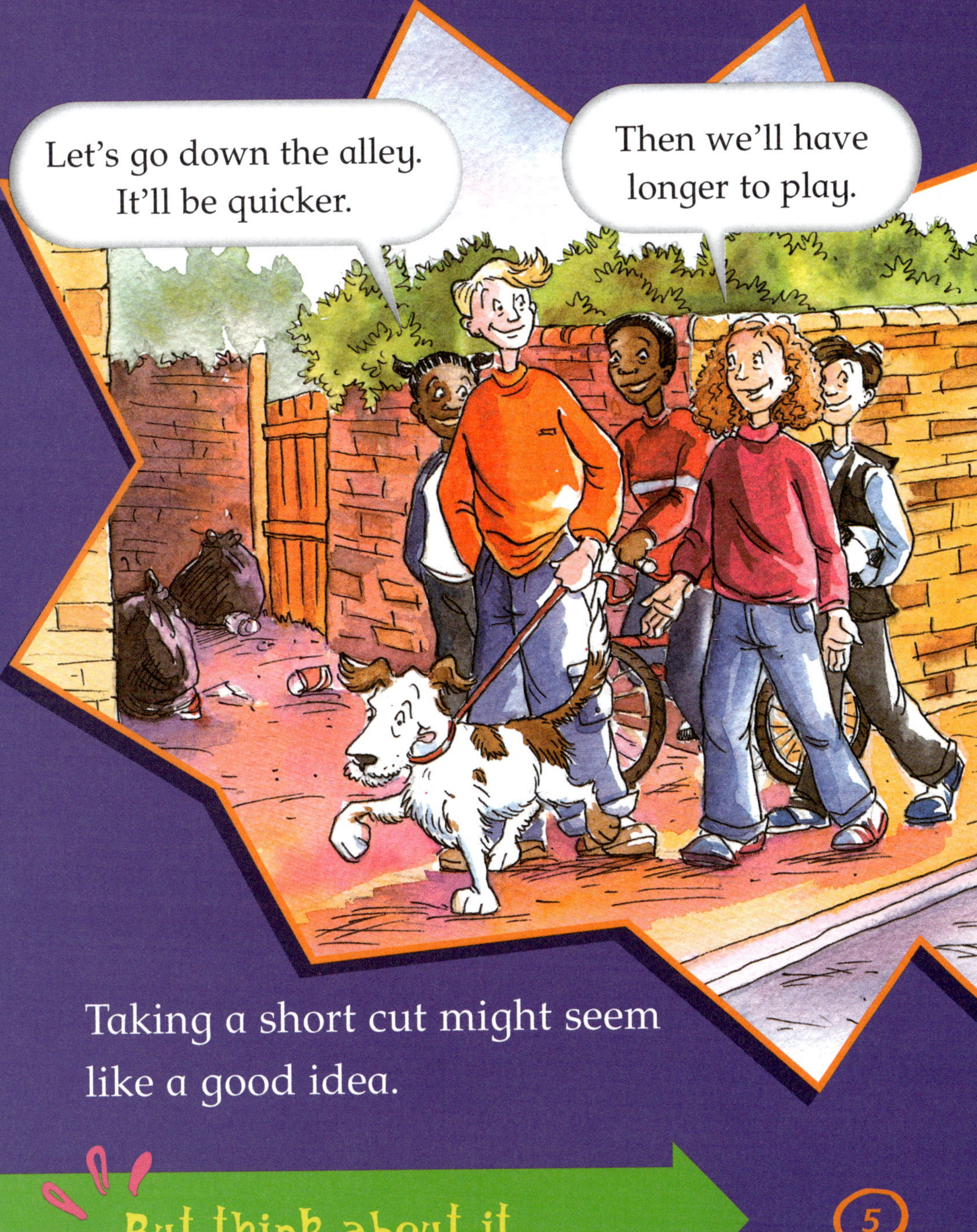


Taking a short cut might seem like a good idea.

But think about it...

5

Your mum or dad may need to find you quickly. They will be worried if you aren't where you said you would be. Also, if you don't keep your promise, your mum or dad might not trust you again. Next time you want to go out on your own, they might say no. So stick to the plan.

6

# On the roads

You might want to play football as you are walking along the road.

If the ball goes into the
road, a car might run
over it.

Or there could be an
accident if a car
swerves to avoid it.

You might have to go
out into the traffic to
get it back.

Even if it doesn't go
in the road, you could
upset and annoy
other people walking
on the pavement.

It might seem like a good idea to
cross the road at the nearest place.

The nearest place might not be safe, because it might be on a bend, or near a turning, or there might be too much traffic. Find the safest place to cross, even if it means you have to walk a bit further.

Over 6 000 children under the age of eleven are hurt walking on the roads every year.

# Near water

On a hot day, you might fancy going for a paddle in a lake or river.

The water could be much deeper than it looks. There could be mud on the bottom, or slippery stones. There could be a strong current. Only go in if you are *sure* the water is shallow enough.



More than 500 people drown in the UK every year, most of them in rivers and lakes.

12

# Things you find

If you find food or drink that has been left or thrown away, you might want to eat it.

But think about it...

13

The food could have been lying around
for days. Germs could have got in.
It could be damp, and mouldy inside.
Poisonous chemicals like weedkillers
might have been sprayed nearby.

Sometimes people tell you to do something naughty or dangerous for a dare. It might seem better to do it than get teased.

But think about it...

If a dare is silly or dangerous, saying no doesn't mean you are scared. It means you are sensible. Don't join in with games you aren't comfortable with.

# Staying together

If your friends are being horrible,
you might want to go off on your own.

What if you can't find
them again later?

What if you have to
go home on your own,
when you told your
mum or dad you would
all stick together?

What if you spend
so long looking for
each other, that
you're all late home?

# Strangers



Most people are nice, kind and friendly. You might be tempted to go with a stranger.

But think about it...

There are a few people who hang around
children because they want to hurt them.
If you really need help from a grown-up,
choose someone yourself. The best person
could be someone who works nearby.

# Time to go

Sometimes something exciting happens just when you're about to leave. You might think a few extra minutes won't make any difference.

But think about it...

Your mum or dad will be worried if you don't arrive home on time. He or she will be angry if you come back late. If you really want to stay, phone and ask if it's all right. Arrange to be home a bit later.

22

# Conclusion

When there are no adults around, you have to decide for yourself what is safe and what is silly. It isn't that difficult. You **do** know how to keep yourself safe …

**if you think about it!**

# index